I0417397

Aubrey the Bee

Written & Illustrated by Shannon Grosheim

Edited by Katie Angst

Many thanks to all my friends and family, especially Yvonne, Eric, and my cousin Katie, who helped me in the creation of this fun book.

May God shower abundant blessings to all who glance upon the pages!

And thank God for all the beautiful plants and the work of our busy, pollinating bees!

Now, let's see what one little bee is up to...

Aubrey the bee buzzes all day

Collecting nectar and

through the town,

pollen from flowers she has found.

To start the day, Aubrey first visits a garden pot overflowing with moss roses.

She delights in the sip of nectar that each rose encloses.

Moss Rose

Petunia

Like her, some nearby petunias wear striking bold stripes, Aubrey discovers.

Though, their streaked petals are different colors.

Aubrey considers herself to be a beautiful black and bright colored insect.

Likewise, she also considers the black-eyed Susan's dark and yellow style perfect.

Black-eyed Susan

She flies further to find the food she fancies,

Among a pretty posse of pleasing purple pansies.

Pansy

Yet the pansies did not offer much

Ahead of her, however, she

nourishment to her liking...

sees petals more inviting...

Petals? Not quite.

Although its rosette arrangement is spectacular, nonetheless...

To the bee's dismay, the "hens and chicks" cactus is flowerless.

Hens & Chicks Cactus

Knockout Roses

Despite Aubrey's difficulty to detect the hues of rouge ahead,

She easily recognizes the yellow center of the flowers in the red knockout rose bed.

Not finding a flower near, Aubrey is a bit discouraged,

That the coleus plant is mostly full of foliage.

Coleus

18

Aubrey zigzags through the garden and finds a zinnia blossom.

It provides plentiful pollen and a drink that tastes awesome!

Zinnia

Cosmos

And on the yummy cosmos,
she meets someone quite familiar.

He calls himself an inchworm,
yet he is really a caterpillar!

On a breeze, Aubrey catches the sweet pea's fragrance she loves so much!

This blossom is an excellent source for a lovely nectar lunch.

Sweet Pea

English Ivy

After a short passing rain, she flies over a large spread of English ivy.

Quickly, she learns that finding flowers here is very unlikely.

Nor does the mushroom provide a single bloom,

Or other food for a bug like Aubrey to consume.

Mushroom

Ground Clover

Then, on the lawn, Aubrey discovers what she simply cannot pass over.

She must visit each flowering head of the pink ground clover!

Dahlia

Then, resting on the petals of the dahlia flower,

Aubrey believes it is only proper to greet her new friend the leafhopper!

Next, she comes across a tree called a blue spruce,

Yet neither pollen nor nectar for her does it produce.

Blue Spruce

Now, Aubrey the bee is feeling more tired

and spent...

But she flies onward

because she smells a new, fresh scent!

Dame's Gillyflower

The small source is surprising.

After all this time, has Aubrey been dreaming?

Or does the Dame's gillyflower smell sweeter in the evening?

With cheer, she finally comes to the last flower of the day!

She delights that the feathery tails of the astilbe (ah-still-bee) **blooms** are not dull and gray.

Astilbe

Aubrey heads back to her home, carrying the pollen with care.

Tomorrow, she'll buzz around again to collect from more flowers elsewhere.

For today, she is done
with her duties in the air.

Now, with all this pollen,
there is honey to prepare!

"The bee collects honey from flowers in such a way as to do the least damage or destruction to them, and he leaves them whole, undamaged and fresh, just as he found them."

- St. Francis de Sales

www.ingramcontent.com/pod-product-compliance
Lightning Source LLC
Chambersburg PA
CBHW060834290526
45792CB00006BB/1924